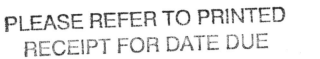

CLASSIFYING ANIMALS

Mammals

Sarah Wilkes

HODDER
Wayland

An imprint of Hodder Children's Books

CLASSIFYING ANIMALS

Titles in this series:

Amphibians Birds Fish Insects Mammals Reptiles

For more information on this series and other Hodder Wayland titles, go to www.hodderwayland.co.uk

Conceived and produced for Hodder Wayland by

Nutshell
MEDIA

www.nutshellmedialtd.co.uk

Consultant: Jane Mainwaring, Natural History Museum
Editor: Polly Goodman
Designer: Tim Mayer
Illustrator: Jackie Harland

Published in Great Britain in 2006 by Hodder Wayland, an imprint of Hodder Children's Books.
© Copyright 2006 Hodder Wayland

The website addresses (URLs) included in this book were valid at the time of going to press. However, because of the nature of the Internet, it is possible that some addresses may have changed, or sites may have changed or closed down since publication. While the author and publishers regret any inconvenience this may cause the readers, no responsibility for any such changes can be accepted by either the author or the publisher.

British Library Cataloguing in Publication Data
Wilkes, Sarah, 1964–
Mammals. – (Classifying animals)
1. Mammals – Classification – Juvenile literature
I. Title
599'.012

ISBN 0 7502 4667 7

Cover photograph: the eyes of a cheetah.
Title page (clockwise from top left): noctule bat; European mole; West Indian manatee; lion.
Chapter openers (from top to bottom): the fur or skin of a giraffe, leopard, elephant, zebra and brown bear.

Picture acknowledgements
Corbis Cover (Marvin Mattelson); **Ecoscene** *Title page top left* (Hugh Clark), *Title page top right* (Steve Austin), *Title page bottom left* (Fritz Pölking), *Title page bottom right* (Phillip Colla), 4 (Owen Newman), 5 (Fritz Pölking), 8 (Michael Maconachie), 9 (Wayne Lawler), 10 (Robin Redfern), 11 (Steve Austin), 12 (Judyth Platt), 13 (Robert Pickett), 17 (Hugh Clark), 18 (Robert Pickett), 19 top (Fritz Pölking), 19 bottom, 20 (Robert Pickett), 21 (Michael Gore), 24 (Peter Cairns), 25, 26 (Robin Redfern), 28, 29, 30, 31 (Phillip Colla), 32, 33, 34, 36 (Fritz Pölking), 37 (Luc Hosten), 38 (Fritz Pölking), 39 (Peter Cairns), 40 (Fritz Pölking), 42 (Karl Ammann), 43 (Robert Pickett); **naturepl.com** 6 (Dave Watts), 7 (Pete Oxford), 14, 16 (Dietmar Nill), 22 (John Downer), 23 (Mark Brownlow), 27 (John Cancalosi), 35 (Eric Baccega), 41 (Anup Shah).

Printed and bound in China.

Hodder Children's Books
A division of Hodder Headline Limited
338 Euston Road, London NW1 3BH

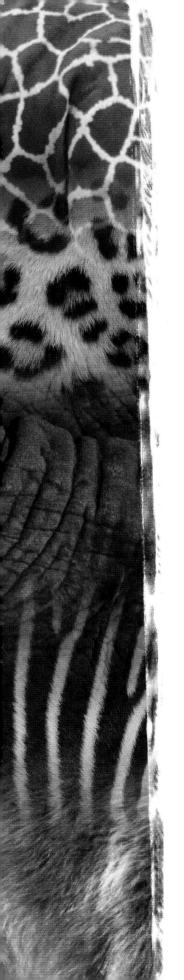

CONTENTS

WHAT ARE MAMMALS?

MAMMALS ARE AMONG THE BEST-known animals in the world. They range from the gigantic blue whale to the tiny pygmy shrew, from bats and hedgehogs to lions and humans.

Mammal features

Mammals are a class of vertebrates. They belong to the phylum Chordata. There are seven other classes of vertebrates, including birds, reptiles and amphibians. All vertebrates have a vertebral column, which is a series of small bones running down their back to provide support. There are about 4,600 species (different types) of mammals, and new species are still being discovered.

Kangaroos are marsupials. This female red kangaroo (**Macropus rufus**) has a joey (young kangaroo) in her pouch.

Mammals have many characteristics in common. The name 'mammal' comes from the mammary glands from which female mammals produce milk for their young. Most mammals are covered in hair and have four types of teeth: incisors, canines, premolars and molars, which are adapted to suit their diet. Internally, all mammals have a sheet of muscle, called the diaphragm, which divides the chest from the abdomen. Mammals are described as being endothermic, or warm blooded. Their body temperature usually stays within a very narrow range, regardless of the outside temperature. For example, the human body temperature is approximately 37 °C (99 °F).

Subclasses

Mammals are divided into three subclasses: monotremes, marsupials and placental mammals (see page 44). Monotremes lay eggs, while marsupials give birth to tiny, immature young that live in their mother's pouch,

CLASSIFICATION

About 2 million different organisms have been identified and sorted into groups, in a process called classification. Biologists look at the similarities and differences between organisms, and group together those with shared characteristics. The largest grouping is the kingdom, for example the animal kingdom. Each kingdom is divided into smaller groups, called phyla (singular: phylum). Each phylum is divided into classes, which are divided into orders, then families, genera (singular: genus), and finally species. A species is a single type of organism with unique features that are different from all other organisms, for example an African elephant. Only members of the same species can reproduce with each other and produce fertile offspring.

The classification of the African elephant (*Loxodonta africana*) is shown on the right.

KINGDOM: Animal

|

PHYLUM: Chordata

|

CLASS: Mammalia

|

ORDER: Proboscidea

|

FAMILY: Elephantidae

|

GENUS: Loxodonta

|

SPECIES: *africana* **(African elephant)**

One way of remembering the order of the different groups is to learn this phrase:
'**K**ings **P**lay **C**hess **O**n **F**ridays **G**enerally **S**peaking'.

feeding on her milk until they are well grown. Placental mammals give birth to well-developed young, some of which can run around within minutes of birth. The subclasses are divided into 26 smaller groups called orders. Mammals in the same order have certain unique features in common.

This books looks at the orders of mammals, their characteristics and the way each group of mammals is adapted to its environment.

The African elephant (*Loxodonta africana*) is a placental mammal and the largest land mammal. Young elephants, called calves, feed on milk for up to three years.

MONOTREMES (MONOTREMATA)

WHEN BIOLOGISTS FIRST studied the duck-billed platypus in 1798, they found it had the beak and webbed feet of a duck and a flat, beaver-like tail. It was like no other animal, so they placed it in an order of its own: Monotremata.

The duck-billed platypus (*Ornithorhynchus anatinus*) uses its webbed feet to propel itself through the water.

Laying eggs

Mammals in the order Monotremata are known as monotremes. They are unusual mammals that lay eggs. There are only three species of monotremes: the duck-billed platypus and two species of echidna, or spiny anteater. Monotremes are found only in Australia (including Tasmania) and New Guinea.

Monotremes have a long snout or bill and, as adults, they have no teeth. The word 'monotreme' means 'one hole', which refers to their one opening, the cloaca. The gut, reproductive and urinary systems all open into the cloaca.

Duck-billed platypus

The platypus is a semi-aquatic animal that lives in streams and rivers. It has a streamlined body and webbed feet. The platypus finds food using its sensitive bill rather than sight. Its thick fur insulates its body against the cold as the water temperature in Australia and New Guinea can fall below freezing in winter.

The female platypus lays one or two soft-shelled eggs in a nest at the end of an underground burrow. She incubates them (keeps them warm) for 10 days until they hatch. The young platypuses feed on milk that oozes out through her fur.

Echidnas

Echidnas are covered in long spines which are used for defence. If threatened by predators, echidnas curl up into a ball, just like hedgehogs. They have small beady eyes and a long, narrow snout. Short-beaked echidnas use their long, sticky tongue to lick up ants and termites. Smell is very important because they use this sense, rather than sight, to locate their prey in the undergrowth. Once a short-beaked echidna locates a nest of ants or termites, it uses its powerful claws to rip the nest open. The long-beaked echidna has a spiny tongue, which it uses to hook earthworms.

Short-beaked echidnas tend to be diurnal, or active during the cooler parts of the day. This is normally at dawn and dusk. However, during the hot summer months they are often nocturnal (active at night). They escape the heat of the day by burying themselves in soft soil.

KEY CHARACTERISTICS
MONOTREMATA

- Lay eggs.
- Eggs hatch after about 10 days.
- Young feed on milk.
- One opening to the outside of their body, called the cloaca.
- Adults do not have teeth.

The echidna (*Tachyglossus aculeatus*) uses its long snout and excellent sense of smell to find its insect prey.

MARSUPIALS (METATHERIA)

MARSUPIALS ARE POUCHED MAMMALS, such as the kangaroo, wombat, opossum, and koala. They are found in Australasia, and in North and South America. Most are forest dwellers, but kangaroos live on grasslands, and possums have moved into towns and cities. Many are nocturnal, appearing only after dusk.

The female koala (*Phascolarctos cinereus*) gives birth to a single offspring, called a joey. When it is six months old, it leaves the pouch and is carried on its mother's back.

Caring for their young

Marsupials are an unusual subclass of mammals. They differ from placental mammals because they give birth to their young after a very short pregnancy. This means that the newborn young are poorly developed and completely dependent on their mother. Most female marsupials have a pouch. Immediately after birth, the tiny babies crawl up their mother's fur into her pouch, where they attach themselves to a teat. They feed on their mother's milk until they are large enough to leave the safety of the pouch. Virginia opossums have huge litters, sometimes in excess of 20, but not all the young survive as the female only has 13 teats. The young opossums ride on their mother's back when they get too big for her pouch.

Getting around

Marsupials use many different methods to move around depending on their habitat. Kangaroos and wallabies live on open grasslands and use their long back legs to hop and jump. Possums, koalas and tree kangaroos live in to grip the bark. The sugar glider is a possum that has folds of skin from the back of the forelimb to the front of the hindlimb. It uses these folds of skin to glide through the air from tree to tree. The wombat and the marsupial mole are burrowing marsupials. Their muscular shoulders and thick neck are ideal for digging.

Marsupial food

Some marsupials, such as koalas, are herbivores, feeding solely on plant foods. However, most marsupials are omnivores. They feed on a mixed diet of plant and animal foods. There are some carnivorous marsupials, including quolls, kowaris and Tasmanian devils. The Tasmanian devil is a fierce hunter, 50–80 cm (20–31 in) long. It preys on insects, small birds and other marsupials.

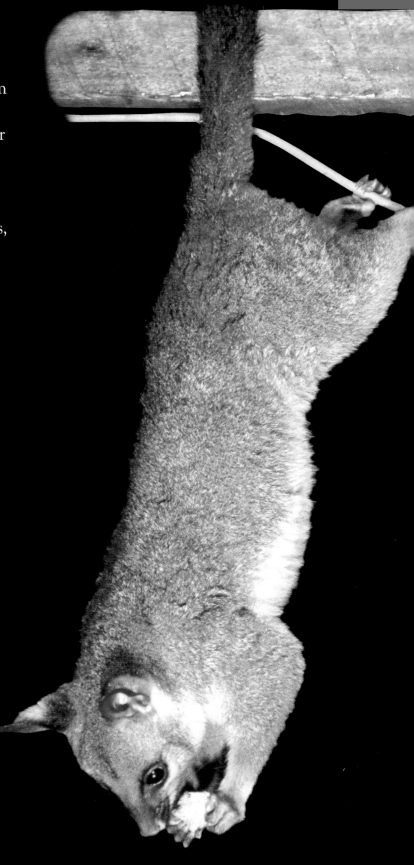

The brush-tailed possum *(Trichosurus vulpecula)* is a common sight in Australian gardens at night. It uses its prehensile tail to help it climb.

KEY CHARACTERISTICS
METATHERIA

- **Young born at an early stage of development.**
- **Presence of a pouch in which young are suckled.**
- **First toe of hind foot is either absent or lacks a claw.**
- **Body temperature is lower than that of placental mammals.**
- **Most marsupials have more teeth than placental mammals.**

INSECTIVORES (INSECTIVORA)

INSECTIVORES ARE SMALL, busy mammals that live all over the world, except for the polar regions and Australasia. They range in size from the tiny pygmy white-toothed shrew, which is just 5 cm (2 in) long and weighs about 2 g (0.07 oz), to the moonrat, which is up to 46 cm (18 in) long and weighs as much as 2 kg (4 lb).

The mole (*Talpa europaea*) has sensitive whiskers on its nose, tail and parts of the body, which help it find its favourite prey – worms.

Insectivores form the third-largest order of mammals after bats and rodents, with about 370 species. The order includes well-known animals such as shrews, moles and hedgehogs as well as the lesser-known solenodons, desmans and tenrecs.

Twitchy noses

Most insectivores are nocturnal and sleep during the day. Shrews are different from most insectivores because they are active during the day. Most insectivores are solitary and live on their own rather than in a group. An insectivore has a pointed head with tiny eyes and ears. Vision is not particularly important to insectivores since they are nocturnal. Instead, they rely on their other senses to find food. The part of the brain that is responsible for an insectivore's sense of smell is particularly large. This gives them an excellent sense of smell and touch, which they use to find prey such as small insects, worms and slugs. One of the most noticeable features of an insectivore is its long, twitchy snout surrounded by sensitive whiskers. The solenodon has a particularly long snout to forage for food in the undergrowth. The star-nosed mole has a strange-looking nose that ends in a mass of pink tentacles, which are very sensitive to touch.

Not just insects

The teeth of insectivores are pointed and suited to crushing the bodies of insects. Although the name insectivore suggests that they eat just insects, they eat a range of other prey too, including worms, snails, slugs and birds' eggs. Water shrews may catch small fish and frogs.

Moving around

Insectivores have four short legs, each of which ends in a foot with five clawed toes. Insectivores are flat-footed, which means they walk with the soles and heels of their feet on the ground. They can walk, run and climb, but they cannot leap. The very rare web-footed tenrec has webbed feet with sharp claws, which help it to swim and to grip slippery rocks.

THE COMMON SHREW

The common shrew (*Sorex araneus*) may be tiny, at only 70 mm (3 in), but it can be quite aggressive, tackling prey many times larger than itself, for example earthworms, slugs and large insects. It must eat up to its own weight in food in each 24-hour period to survive. It has about 10 bursts of frantic hunting activity each day, when it searches for food, and then it rests.

The common shrew (*Sorex araneus*) has a pointed head with a long snout and tiny eyes. The ears are tiny and not visible through its fur.

Adaptation to habitat

Insectivores are specially adapted to their habitats in different ways. The mole, for example, is adapted to living underground. Its body is streamlined for digging and it has huge front paws with long claws, ideally suited to digging out tunnels. Its short, thick fur can lie at any angle, allowing the animal to move forwards or backwards in a tight tunnel. The mole is virtually blind, so instead of using sight, it uses its whiskers and sense of smell to locate worms and other animals that fall into the tunnels.

Hedgehogs (*Erinaceus europeaus*) have long spines which they use for defence. When under attack, they curl up into a tight ball, with the spines sticking out.

Surviving winter

Hedgehogs cannot find enough food in winter to survive, so they go into a deep sleep called hibernation. During the autumn months, they build up their fat reserves by eating lots of food. Then they make a nest for themselves under a pile of leaves and hibernate. During hibernation, hedgehogs' body temperatures fall from about 38 °C (100 °F) to just 4 °C (39 °F), which means that they do not have to use much energy to keep warm. Their heart beats slowly and they only breathe a few times every minute. When the temperature rises in the spring, the hedgehogs' body temperatures rise and they wake up.

Poisonous bite

The European water shrew, the North American short-tailed shrew and the solenodon use a poisonous bite for defence and to stun their prey. These insectivores and the male platypus are the only poisonous mammals. Solenodons are very rare. They are only found on two islands in the Caribbean – Cuba and Hispaniola. Their numbers have been decreasing because they live in forests that have been cleared for farmland. They have also been killed by animals such as dogs, cats, rats and mongooses, which are not native to the islands.

Extra orders: tree shrews, elephant shrews and colugos

Three groups of mammals, the tree shrews, elephant shrews and colugos (flying lemurs), used to be classified in the same order as insectivores, but now each has been placed in a separate order. Tree shrews are small, squirrel-like mammals that have well-developed senses. They feed on small animals such as insects. Elephant shrews, as their name suggests, have a long and very sensitive snout. They have powerful back legs and can run quickly along the ground. Colugos use a wing-like flap of skin that stretches between their limbs to glide between trees.

Tree shrews are small, secretive mammals. Food passes quickly through their simple gut so they have to eat for much of the day to survive.

KEY CHARACTERISTICS
INSECTIVORA

- Long snout with wet nose and whiskers.
- Presence of a cloaca.
- Five toes on each foot.
- Flat footed.
- Relatively small brains compared with other mammals.

BATS (CHIROPTERA)

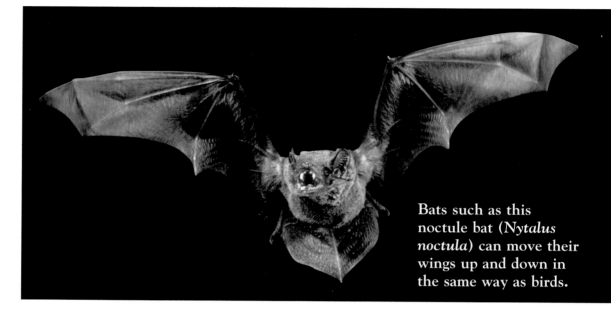

Bats such as this noctule bat (*Nytalus noctula*) can move their wings up and down in the same way as birds.

BATS ARE THE ONLY MAMMALS THAT CAN FLY. SOME mammals, such as colugos and sugar gliders, use a flap of skin to glide from tree to tree, but only bats can flap their wings.

Most bats are nocturnal, so people see them less than other mammals. There are, however, 1,000 species of bats and they are found all over the world except for the polar regions. The order is divided into two suborders: Megachiroptera (large bats) and Microchiroptera (small bats). Megachiroptera is made up of one large family of 166 species of fruit bat. The Microchiroptera contains 16 families of mainly insect-eating bats.

Adapted for flight

Bats are specially adapted for flight in a number of ways. The word *chiroptera* means 'hand wing', which relates to the bat's wings. The wings are formed from skin stretched between the fingers and the body. The forelimb of the bat is different from that of other mammals. Some of its finger bones are as long as the bone in its forearm. These elongated fingers support the wing, holding it out in flight. Also, bats have a small, lightweight body, which means they have less weight to carry when they fly. Bats hang by their legs when they rest. But for anything other than hanging, their legs are weak and their knee bends backwards rather than forwards, as in other mammals. This means that many bats, especially the larger species, cannot walk on the ground.

Echolocation

Bats have well-developed senses. Megachiroptera bats hunt using sight and smell. They have large eyes to gather as much light as possible, which gives them good eyesight. Microchiroptera bats do not rely on sight. They use an unusual ability called echolocation to navigate in the dark and find food. The bats send out clicks from their voice box through their nose or mouth. Sound waves bounce off objects or prey in their path and come back to the bats as echoes. These bats can even identify the size and shape of an object by the sound of its echo. Some bats have a peculiar-looking fleshy structure, called a nose-leaf, above their nose, which helps to direct the sounds.

KEY CHARACTERISTICS
CHIROPTERA

- **The only mammals that can fly.**
- **Four elongated fingers support the skin that forms the wing.**
- **Thumb has a claw.**
- **Legs are weak and the knee bends backwards.**
- **Teeth adapted to diet.**
- **Most have excellent hearing and about half use echolocation.**

In echolocation, the bat produces sounds that bounce off objects. The echoes are picked up by the bat's ears.

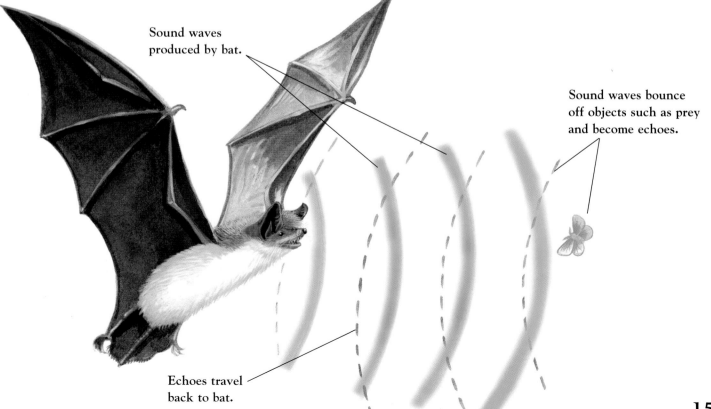

Sound waves produced by bat.

Sound waves bounce off objects such as prey and become echoes.

Echoes travel back to bat.

15

Pollination

Bats are important pollinators of flowers, including those of fruit trees. Fruit bats feed on fruits and the nectar of flowers using their extra-long tongue to reach deep into the flower. When they visit a flower to drink nectar they pick up pollen, which they carry to other flowers. This allows the flower to produce seeds. Bats also have a role in dispersing the seeds of these plants. When the bats eat fruit, the seeds pass through their gut and out in their droppings.

Bat food

Microchiroptera bats eat a variety of foods, especially insects such as nocturnal moths and mosquitoes, which they catch in mid-flight. Fisherman bats take fish from rivers, scooping up fish lying at the surface with their long claws. The vampire bat feeds on blood. This bat flies at dusk, looking for a suitable animal such as a bird, horse, cow or even a human. It lands beside the animal and crawls over to it on its weak legs. The bat then removes any feathers or hair covering the skin before biting the flesh. Its incisor teeth at the front of its mouth are very thin and pointed, so they slip easily through the skin without the victim noticing. The bat then sucks blood for about 30 minutes. The blood does not clot because the bat's saliva contains an anti-clotting substance.

A vampire bat (*Desmodus rotundus*) licks the blood as it oozes from the bite on a chicken's leg.

This insect-eating noctule bat (*Nytalus noctula*) rests by hanging from its feet.

Roosting and hibernation

Since bats are nocturnal, they spend the day resting in a roost, often with many other bats. The roost may be a loft, hollow tree or cave. These places are safe from predators and sheltered from the weather. Tent-building bats build their own roost by biting through the large leaves of a palm or banana tree so that they fold over, creating a tent. As many as 50 or so bats may shelter under the tent. Fruit bats often roost in caves and at dusk they stream out of the cave in search of food. Some bats hibernate through cold winters because if they did not, they would not find enough food to survive. They come out of hibernation when the weather gets warmer.

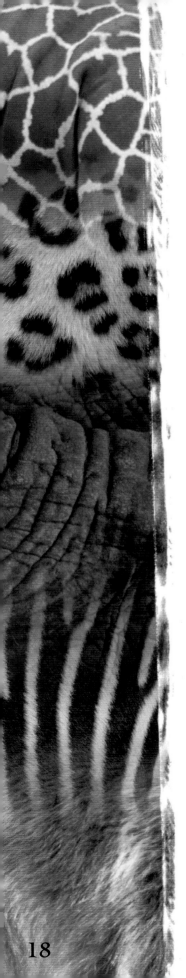

PRIMATES (PRIMATE)

MONKEYS, LEMURS, APES and humans all belong to the order of primates. Apes, such as chimpanzees and gorillas, are our closest living relatives. There are about 180 species of primates and most live in forests in the warmer parts of the world.

Primates have a well-developed brain and are more intelligent than other mammals. They have two large, forward-facing eyes, which allow them to have three-dimensional vision and be able to judge distances. Most have nails rather than claws on their fingers and toes. The primates are divided into two groups: Stepsirhini (lemurs, lorises, pottos and bushbabies) and the Haplorhini (the higher primates such as monkeys and apes).

Stepsirhini
These are the small primates with a dog-like face, such as the lemur and the bushbaby.

Lemurs, such as this Coquerel's dwarf lemur (*Mirza coquerel*), are only found on the tropical island of Madagascar.

KEY CHARACTERISTICS
PRIMATE
- Well-developed brain.
- Forward-facing eyes for 3D vision.
- Most have hands and feet adapted for grasping.
- Most have flat nails rather than claws.

Animals in this group have large eyes with excellent night vision. They live in trees, so their hands and feet are adapted for gripping.

Monkeys

Monkeys can be divided into two large groups: New World and Old World monkeys. It is the shape of the nose that distinguishes these two groups. New World monkeys, such as marmosets and howlers, are found in South America. Their nostrils are wide open, far apart and face outwards. Many have a prehensile tail, which acts like a fifth limb and is able to grip branches. The tail helps the monkey to balance and grip as it travels through the trees. Old World monkeys are found in Africa and Asia, and include baboons and macaques. Their nostrils are narrow, close together and point downwards. They do not have a prehensile tail and their bottom has a thick 'sitting pad' – a bit like a cushion!

Apes

The apes include gibbons, chimpanzees, bonobos, gorillas, orang-utans and humans. These primates have the largest brains, especially humans, so the apes are more intelligent than the other primates. Most apes have a broad chest with a shoulder that allows a great deal of movement. Their arms are longer than their legs. Their face is flattened and has powerful jaws. The apes do not have a tail. Their hands are grasping and they have opposable thumbs and toes. This means that the thumb sticks out at an angle so they can grip and manipulate objects. Chimpanzees and gorillas also have an opposable big toe.

(Above) The foot of the gorilla has a large gap between the big toe and the other toes so it can be used to grip food and objects.

(Below) Mature male Western lowland gorillas (*Gorilla gorilla*) like this one, have silver-grey hairs across their back and are often called silverbacks.

19

The spider monkey (*Ateles geoffroyi*) uses its long, prehensile tail as a fifth limb to grip branches as it swings through trees.

Adaptation to habitat

Most primates live in forests and they are well adapted to this habitat. Small monkeys can run along the branches of trees. Heavier primates tend to have long limbs and they hang from branches rather than run along them. For example, the spider monkeys of South America wrap their prehensile tail around branches to provide balance and grip, and to swing from branch to branch. Gibbons have a style of movement called brachiation, which means they swing from hand to hand through the forest. Orang-utans also have long limbs, but they have a heavier body so they climb through the trees.

Living in groups

Most primates are social animals that live in family groups, with the exception of the orang-utan, some lemurs and bushbabies. A family group is usually made up of one or two males, a number of females and their young of varying ages. Primates usually have one or two offspring at a time. They care for their young for a long period, teaching them the skills they will need as adults. Other members of the group will look after and defend the youngsters. Some primates, such as chimpanzees and spider monkeys, live in large groups of up to 200 individuals, which split from time to time into a number of smaller groups.

Defending a territory

Primates are territorial. They live in a particular area of a forest, which they will defend from others crossing the boundaries. Smaller primates such as lemurs make sure that the boundaries of their territory are marked with their scent. Others advertise their presence using sound. The booming calls of the howler monkeys and siamang gibbons travel many kilometres through the forest every morning.

Active at night

Most monkeys and apes, like humans, are active during the day and sleep at night. Chimpanzees, gorillas and other apes sleep in a nest of branches and leaves raised off the forest floor, which they make during the day. However, most lemurs, lorises and bushbabies are nocturnal. Apart from moon- and starlight, there is little light at night and these mammals have eyes that are especially adapted to cope with nocturnal life. A special layer at the back of their eyes, called the reflective tapetum, bounces light back out, giving them better night vision. Tarsiers have exceptionally large, dish-like eyes to capture as much night light as possible.

BIGGEST AND SMALLEST

The gorilla is the largest primate. Male gorillas stand 1.9 m (6.2 ft) tall and weigh as much as 200 kg (441 lb). The smallest primate is the red mouse lemur. Its body is barely 10 cm (4 in) long, and it has a tail 5 cm (2 in) long. It weighs 35 g (1 oz). The pygmy marmoset is the smallest monkey. It is so small that it would fit inside a teacup.

These Japanese snow monkeys (*Macaque japonensis*) are grooming each other to keep their fur clean and remove parasites such as ticks and fleas.

ANTEATERS, SLOTHS AND ARMADILLOS (XENARTHRA)

The three-toed sloth (*Bradypus sp.*) hangs upside down from a tree using its hooked claws. Its thick fur is often home to algae, mites, ticks and beetles.

ANTEATERS, SLOTHS AND armadillos are some of the most unusual mammals. Although these three animals look very different from each other, they are grouped in the order Xenarthra because of the arrangement of extra bones in their lower back.

Xenarthra features

The order Xenarthra contains 29 species, most of which are found in Central and South America. The nine-banded armadillo also lives in North America. The extra bones in the back of members of this order give added strength and support. This support is essential to anteaters and armadillos because they dig using their powerful forelimbs equipped with long claws. The sloth needs the extra support because it spends most of the day hanging from its claws in the trees.

Armour plating

The armadillo family is covered by hard armour plating. The plates are actually hardened skin that cover the head, back, sides and limbs. There are bands around the middle of the plating to give the armadillos flexibility, so they can roll up for protection. The number of bands varies between different species. The giant armadillo has an extra-large third claw on its front limbs, which it uses to rip up soil to find food.

Diet

Members of the Xenarthra order have either small, unspecialized teeth or, in the case of the anteater, no teeth at all. Armadillos and anteaters are mostly insectivores, feeding on termites and other insects, small birds and rodents. Sloths are herbivores. They eat leaves, shoots, twigs and fruit. Sloths spend most of their time feeding and when their stomach is full, it makes up one third of their total body weight. The plants they eat are low in nutritional content and the digestion of the leaves takes weeks, so sloths live very slow lives.

This Brazilian three-banded armadillo (*Tolypeutes tricinctus*) is curled up in a protective ball.

Extra orders: pangolins and aardvarks

Pangolins have a similar body shape to armadillos, but they are not closely related. They belong to the order Pholidota. They have a body covered by scales made from hardened hair. They do not have any teeth but their tongue is long and sticky – ideal for collecting ants and termites. Aardvarks belong to the order Tubulidentata. They lack any body armour but they are powerful diggers, able to dig out burrows more than 10 m (33 ft) long. Aardvarks have a pig-like face with a long snout and large ears. Their teeth are adapted to crushing hard-backed insects for food.

RODENTS (RODENTIA)

RODENTS ARE GNAWING ANIMALS such as rats, mice and squirrels. This order is the most varied and widespread of all mammals, found in almost all habitats from deserts and grasslands to forests and marshes. They even live in the cold Arctic. In fact, there are more than 2,000 different types of rodents – that's 40 per cent of all mammals.

Squirrels, such as this red squirrel (*Scuirus vulgaris*), have a cylindrical-shaped body and a bushy tail, which is used for balance. They handle food in their front paws.

KEY CHARACTERISTICS
RODENTIA

- Four sharp incisors that grow continuously.
- No canine teeth but a space called the diastema.
- Most walk on the soles of their feet.
- Keen sense of smell and hearing.
- Have whiskers.

Rodent features

The order Rodentia can be divided into three main groups: squirrel-like rodents, mouse-like rodents and cavy-like rodents.

The main feature of rodents is their gnawing ability – a result of their incisor teeth and powerful jaws. At the front of their mouth they have four sharp, chisel-like incisors that can gnaw through the toughest materials. The teeth get worn down but they are replaced by new growth because the incisors never stop growing. This is because the root of the tooth is open, rather than closed as in other mammals. Rodents do not have any canine teeth but molars at the back of their mouth grind their food. They have extra-large jaw muscles to give them a powerful bite. Other features include their long tail, short legs with clawed toes, well-developed senses and long whiskers.

Reproduction

Most rodents have an ability to reproduce quickly and produce several offspring per litter, with the exception of the larger capybara and mara. Some species of vole can produce 13 litters in a single year. Many are ready to breed by the time they are two months old so their reproductive rate is very high.

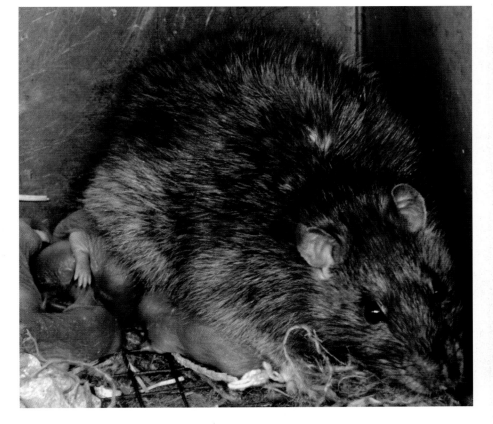

Pests

Many rodent species are classed as pests, particularly rats and mice. These rodents live close to people and are linked with disease; for example, fleas that live on rats helped to spread bubonic plague. Each year, rats and mice contaminate millions of tonnes of human food with their urine and faeces. Traditionally they are killed using poisons but, increasingly, rodents are becoming resistant to the poisons and controlling them is more difficult.

Rodents such as this brown rat (*Rattus norvegicus*) give birth to tiny pink babies that lack hair and must be cared for in a nest. The young leave the nest when they are 21–28 days old.

Adaptation to habitat

Rodents are very adaptable animals. Rats, for example, have hitch-hiked with humans as they explored the world and today they are found everywhere except the polar regions. The rat's success is due to the fact that it is an opportunist. It feeds on a wide range of plant foods, such as seeds, fruits and vegetables, as well as the food waste of humans. It has excellent senses and is able to detect food stored inside buildings. It is also incredibly agile and able to climb up ropes and walls to gain entry to buildings and ships.

Building homes

Some rodents build elaborate homes. Squirrels build large dreys in trees, using leaves and branches. Prairie dogs excavate an underground network of tunnels, known as a town, on grassland. They use the tunnels to escape predators and to raise their young. Some rodents have actually transformed the landscape in which they live. Beavers, for example, use their teeth to fell branches and small trees to construct dams across rivers. This creates a lake that may flood a whole valley. Once the new lake is deep enough they build their home, called a lodge, in the middle.

Surviving the cold

Rodents have a number of different ways of surviving cold weather. Mountain rodents such as the chinchilla, which lives in the Andes, have very thick fur to protect them from the cold. Other rodents, such as dormice, woodchucks and marmots, survive the winter by hibernating. They find a safe, dry nest site in which to hibernate through the winter.

The ship rat or black rat (*Rattus rattus*) can climb ropes. This means it can board ships and be carried around the world.

Extra order: lagomorphs

Rabbits may look like rodents, with their long, sharp incisors, but they are classified in a separate order called Lagomorpha. The word 'Lagomorpha' means 'hare-shaped'. There are 44 species in this order, which is made up of rabbits, hares and pikas. Like rodents, lagomorphs have continually growing incisors, but they also have a second pair of small incisors, known as peg incisors.

Rabbits and hares have large ears and long back legs, which help them detect and run away from danger. They are the prey of many predators so they are well adapted for quick movement. Some hares can run at speeds of up to 48 km/h (28 mph). Pikas are smaller than rabbits and hares. They look a bit like a guinea pig, with rounded ears and short legs. Pikas live high up in the mountains and underground in deserts in North America, eastern Europe, the Himalayas and northern Asia.

The long ears of this black-tailed jack rabbit (*Lepus californicus*) give it excellent hearing, which it uses to detect approaching predators.

CAPYBARAS

The largest rodents are the capybaras of South America, which weigh up to 64 kg (141 lb). Capybaras are a bit like hippos. They spend the day wallowing in water and feeding on water plants, emerging at night to feed on grass and crops. When a predator approaches, the capybaras produce an alarm call and rush into the water, where they form a tight group. The young are safe in the centre while the adults stand around them facing out.

WHALES, DOLPHINS AND PORPOISES (CETACEA)

WHALES, DOLPHINS AND PORPOISES BELONG TO THE order Cetacea and are called cetaceans. They evolved from land mammals millions of years ago and are the only mammals, other than manatees and dugongs (see page 31), that live their entire lives in the water. Cetaceans even give birth to their young in the water.

The female humpback whale (*Megaptera novaeangliea*) gives birth to a single calf under water and pushes it to the surface to take its first breath.

Cetacean features

Cetaceans breathe in air through a blowhole on the top of their head that leads to the lungs, unlike fish, which breathe using gills. They have sleek, streamlined bodies that slip through the water with ease. They have almost no hair as this would slow them down. They have no hind limbs and their forelimbs are modified to form flippers. Cetaceans swim by moving their muscular tail up and down. Their tail fluke lies horizontal in the water, whereas the tail fin of the fish lies vertically. Killer whales and shortfin pilot whales are the fastest cetaceans, swimming at up to 48 km/h (30 mph).

Two groups

There are over 77 species of cetaceans, which are divided into two groups: baleen whales and toothed whales. Baleen whales include the blue, fin, humpback, right and sei whales. Instead of teeth, these whales have baleen plates in their mouth which they use to filter small fish from the water. The toothed whales include the dolphins, killer and sperm whales. Their teeth are cone-shaped and point back into the mouth. This is an adaptation to eating fish as it stops the fish from getting away.

Social behaviour

Cetaceans have very strong relationships between each other, and the strongest tie is between mother and calf. The adults care for their young for at least a year. Many cetaceans travel in groups, called pods. The toothed whales often hunt their prey in pods, migrate together and even share the care of their young.

Whales and dolphins are very acrobatic and many jump out of the water. This is called breaching, and they slap the water as they come down. Biologists are unsure why whales breach – it may be for play, to knock off skin parasites or for communication. Spy-hopping is another cetacean activity in which the mammal pokes its head out of the water to take a look around. Lobtailing is when whales stick their tail out of the water and then slap it on the water's surface to make a very loud sound. This may be a warning to the other whales in the group.

KEY CHARACTERISTICS
CETACEA

- **Virtually hairless.**
- **Streamlined body with forelimbs modified to form flippers.**
- **Horizontal tail flukes.**
- **No hind limbs.**
- **Elongated head that merges with the body with no obvious neck.**
- **No external ears.**

Dolphins, such as these common dolphins (*Delphinus delphis*), often travel together in large groups and may work together to capture shoals of fish.

Migration

Many cetaceans, especially baleen whales, migrate over very long distances each year. They travel, sometimes in pods, from cold-water feeding grounds to warm-water breeding grounds. For example, gray whales spend the summer months in the Arctic Ocean and Bering Sea, before swimming down the warmer Pacific coast of North America to Southern California and Mexico, where they spend the winter.

A blue whale (*Balaenoptera musculus*) and her calf swim along the coast of California on their annual migration to their winter feeding grounds in the Arctic.

Finding food

Baleen whales are filter feeders. They feed on the plankton, krill and fish in the water. They gulp huge mouthfuls of water into their mouth and then push it out through their baleen plates, sieving the food.

Toothed whales are predators, hunting their food. They chase prey such as squid, octopus and fish. Killer whales hunt seals, penguins and other whales, too. Dolphins and killer whales often work together to herd their prey in order to trap them. The sperm whale hunts for squid and giant octopus, which live in deep water. Most dives are between 300 and 600 m (1,000–2,000 ft), but sperm whales may be able to dive as deep as 3,000 m (10,000 ft). They can survive under water for up to two hours in order to reach such depths.

The toothed whales find their prey using echolocation, just like bats. They emit high-frequency clicks that bounce off objects in their path. They also use the echoes to navigate in murky water.

Communicating

Whales communicate with each other using sound. Baleen whales sing low-frequency songs that are thought to attract a mate and to help them keep track of members of the pod. The most well known is the song of the humpback whale, which lasts up to 30 minutes and can be heard over great distances. Beluga whales also sing to keep in contact and they are nicknamed the 'sea canaries'. They produce a range of sounds including moos, chirps and whistles. Some of these sounds can even be heard in the air. Sperm whales produce clicks. Individual sperm whales produce a particular pattern of clicks called 'codas', which they repeat at intervals.

Extra order: Sirenia

Dugongs and manatees may look a bit like whales, but they are placed in the order Sirenia. There are three species of manatee and one species of dugong. They are all large, slow-moving mammals that feed solely on plants. They have paddle-like front limbs and a flat, broad tail, which they use to propel them through the water.

BIGGEST AND SMALLEST

The blue whale is the largest animal that has ever lived. It grows to about 29 m (95 ft) long – the height of a nine-storey building – and weighs as much as 25 bull elephants. These enormous animals eat about 4 tonnes of krill each day. Adult blue whales have no predators except humans. The smallest whale is the dwarf sperm whale, which as an adult is only 2.6 m (8.5 ft) long.

Manatees, such as this West Indian manatee (*Trechechus manatus*), are found in shallow water where there is plenty of their favourite food – sea grass.

CARNIVORES (CARNIVORA)

LIONS, WOLVES, FOXES and bears are all members of the order of Carnivora. The word 'carnivore' is often defined as 'an animal that eats meat'. However, many carnivores in this order do not eat just meat. These mammals are grouped together because of features of their anatomy that are linked to their diet.

There are approximately 230 species in the order Carnivora. Among this order are the smaller members, the weasels and stoats, civets and mongooses, as well as the larger ones, such as brown bears and tigers. There are some amphibious species, too. Seals and walruses live in the sea and come on to land to give birth to their pups. Otters usually hunt in water but spend the rest of their time on land. Some otters live in freshwater rivers, while sea otters live in coastal waters such as those along the Pacific coast of North America.

Giant pandas (*Ailuropoda melanoleuca*) are herbivores as they feed mostly on bamboo shoots. They have an enlarged wrist bone that sticks out, helping them to grip bamboo stems.

Teeth and claws

The main feature of carnivores is their specialized teeth, which are adapted to a diet of eating mostly meat. Their teeth have to be able to grip and tear the flesh of their prey. They have small incisors at the front of the mouth for gripping and for nibbling bits of meat off bone, and for grooming their fur. There are four long, curved canines, which stab and grab their prey. Behind the canines are the large premolars and molars with jagged edges that are used for slicing through flesh. The fourth upper premolar and the first lower molar are larger than the others, and are called carnassials. Carnivores have powerful jaw muscles, which are essential for holding on to and biting into prey animals. They swallow chunks of food without chewing, so their stomachs are adapted to digesting large pieces of meat.

Carnivores have four or five long, curved claws on each foot. In cats, the claws can be retracted (withdrawn) so that they can creep up silently on their prey. Cats use their claws to lock on to and pull down prey.

Well-developed senses

Most carnivores are predators, so they have well-developed senses for locating their prey. They have excellent eyesight and hearing, and a good sense of smell. Some have whiskers around their nose for touch. Their forward-facing eyes provide 3D vision, which is essential for judging distances. Many carnivores are better at detecting movement than seeing detail. A well-camouflaged prey animal may not be spotted until it moves.

KEY CHARACTERISTICS
CARNIVORA

- Four large canine teeth for stabbing and gripping prey.
- Four carnassial teeth for shearing through meat and bone.
- Well-developed senses, especially sight and hearing.
- Four or five toes with sharp claws.

The large canines are clearly visible when a carnivore such as this lion (*Panthera leo*) opens its mouth.

Hunting together

The survival of a carnivore depends on whether it can catch enough food. Older or sick individuals often starve to death because they are not able to catch prey. They may be forced to scavenge for food or attack easy prey such as people. Some carnivores, such as lions and wolves, work together to catch food while others, such as tigers and foxes, prefer to hunt alone.

Lions live in groups called prides on the open savannahs of southern and eastern Africa. A pride consists of an adult male, several lionesses and their cubs. The lionesses work together to catch prey. One lioness approaches the prey animals, forcing them to move towards the other lionesses who are lying in wait. Lions have to get closer to their prey without being spotted than other predators, such as the cheetah, since they cannot run as far or as fast. However, several lionesses together can bring down large prey such as wildebeest and cape buffalo.

Lionesses (*Panthera leo*) creep to within 30 m (98 ft) of their prey before they charge, pulling it down with their claws before giving a deadly bite to the throat. These lionesses are pulling down a young cape buffalo (*Syncerus caffer*).

SEALS AND SEA LIONS

Walruses, seals and sea lions are adapted to living in water, but the females must come on to land to give birth to their pups. True seals have no external ears and their back flippers point backwards. Sea lions and fur seals have small external ears and back flippers that can be twisted forwards for moving on land. Walruses have a distinctive pair of tusks. Only walruses and eared seals can support themselves on their front flippers when they come on to land.

Feeding on salmon

The grizzly or brown bear is the largest land carnivore. It feeds on a wide-ranging diet that includes insects and small mammals as well as roots and fungi. However, in the autumn the brown bear needs to eat fatty food so it can build up enough body fat ready for its winter sleep. Many brown bears can be found along rivers in the autumn, feeding on the salmon migrating upstream to breed. Salmon is rich in protein and fat, and the bears can put on a lot of weight by eating it.

Surviving the cold

Some carnivores survive the extreme cold of the polar regions. They are the polar bear, Arctic fox, walrus, and some of the seals and sea lions. The Weddell seal, for example, can cope with an air temperature of –40 °C (–40 °F) while lying on the ice. The bodies of these polar mammals are specially adapted so that they retain as much of their body heat as possible. As well as thick fur, they have a layer of blubber (fat) beneath the skin. Polar bears also have black skin which absorbs more heat, and hollow hairs that help to conduct sunlight straight to their skin.

Brown or grizzly bears (*Ursus arctos*) feast on salmon in the autumn to build up their body fat before they go into their winter hibernation.

ELEPHANTS (PROBOSCIDEA)

These young African bull elephants (*Loxodonta africana*) are carrying out mock fights.

THE LARGEST LAND ANIMAL is the African elephant. Today there are just three species of elephant, but in prehistoric times there may have been more than 300 different species. Elephants are long-lived mammals with some individuals reaching 70 to 80 years of age.

Giant plant eaters

Elephants belong to the order Proboscidea. The three species are the African, African forest and Asian elephant. They are all plant eaters. The African elephant lives on the African savannah. The African forest elephant is found in the dense forests of eastern Africa, while the Asian elephant is widespread across India and Southeast Asia, in mostly forest habitats.

Trunks, tusks and ears

One of the most noticeable features of the elephant is its trunk. The trunk is long and muscular, and formed from the upper lip and nose. Elephants use their trunk like a fifth limb for touching, handling food and drinking water. Their huge teeth are flat with ridges and ideal for grinding plant material. Elephants have six sets of teeth during their lifetime, with each set being made up of four huge teeth. There are two teeth in the upper jaw and two in the lower jaw. Elephant tusks are elongated upper incisor teeth. They first appear when the elephant is two years old and continue to grow throughout its life. All elephants have tusks, but the tusks of the female Asian elephants are very small and do not protrude beyond the lips. Elephant ears are large too, especially those of the African elephant. They are well supplied with blood vessels and flapping the ears helps to keep the animal cool.

Living in herds

Elephants live in herds, with the adult males and females living separately. Female elephants live together in family groups led by the oldest female, known as the matriarch. The bull elephants leave the family group and live either with other bulls or on their own. They only join the females to breed. When a male elephant is ready to breed, he is said to have come into musk and is quite aggressive to other bulls.

Adapting to their environment

Some African elephants live in semi-desert areas of south-west Africa. They have slightly longer legs that allow them to walk longer distances in search of water. Some elephants have learnt to use their tusks to dig for salt in caves. The forest elephant looks very similar to the African elephant, although it is slightly shorter. Being smaller, it can move through the dense forest more easily.

Extra order: Hyracoidea (rock and bush hyraxes)

The hyrax is one of the closest living relatives to the elephant, although it looks nothing like an elephant. Both the hyrax and the elephant have ridged teeth, similar foot bones and flat nails on their toes. Hyraxes have long incisor teeth that continue to grow and a scent gland on their back.

KEY CHARACTERISTICS
PROBOSCIDEA

- Trunk formed from upper lip and nose.
- Tusks formed from the upper incisors.
- Skeleton made of heavy bones to support the animal's great weight.
- Large, fan-shaped ears that help heat loss.

The rock hyrax (*Procavia capensis*) is a small, brown mammal that lives in rocky outcrops, where it feeds on plants.

UNGULATES (PERISSODACTYLA AND ARTIODACTYLA)

The black rhino (*Diceros bicornis*) has an odd number of toes. It has a prehensile upper lip to browse on the twigs and new shoots of bushes and low trees.

UNGULATES IS THE GENERAL NAME given to a large group of mammals that have hooves. Hooves are modified toe nails, which help ungulates to run fast.

Two orders

Ungulates are divided into two orders: Perissodactyla and Artiodactyla. Members of Perissodactyla have an odd number of toes, either one or three. This order contains 17 species of horses, zebras, tapirs and rhinos. Artiodactyls have an even number of toes, either two or four. There are more than 200 species of even-toed artiodactyls, including pigs, camels, llamas, deer, giraffe, sheep and goats.

Ungulate features

Ungulates have four long limbs, with bones arranged in a different way from other mammals. The bones in ungulates' feet are very long and fused together. The foot is held in such a way that only the very tips of the toes touch the ground. Millions of years ago, each toe ended in a hoof. Over time, the feet evolved so that some of the toes fused together. Present-day ungulates have between one and four toes. The edge of the hoof is thickened with a tough material called keratin, so it is strong enough to support the weight of the animal's body. Keratin is the same material that forms hair and nails.

Teeth and digestion

Ungulates have long jaws with teeth adapted to eating plants, especially grass. The teeth are large and ridged so they can grind food. Many artiodactyls are ruminant animals. These are animals with a stomach that has three or four chambers. They chew and swallow their food before regurgitating it back into their mouth so they can chew it again. This means that the food is well broken down and can be digested more easily. Ruminants also have micro-organisms in their stomach to help digest the tough plant food.

Horns, antlers and tusks

Many ungulates have bony outgrowths such as horns and antlers on their head, which they use as weapons. Antelope and cattle have permanent horns with bone in the middle. Deer have antlers that are also made from bone, but they are shed each year and replaced by a new set. As a deer gets older, the antlers get larger. Pigs and hippos have tusks – large teeth that grow from their jawbones, which can be seen on the sides of their face. The tusks are used for fighting, defence or digging up roots. The rhino's horn is very different. It is made from compressed hairs rather than bone.

The red deer stag (*Cervus elaphus*) has an impressive set of branched antlers, which are shed and regrown each year. During the breeding season the stags fight, locking their antlers with their heads down. Then they push and twist each other until one gives up.

BIGGEST AND SMALLEST

- The largest ungulate is the white rhino, which is 4 m (13 ft) long and weighs up to 2.3 tonnes.

- The smallest ungulate is the lesser mouse deer, which is 48 cm (19 in) long and weighs just 2.5 kg (5.5 lb).

- The pronghorn antelope is one of the fastest long-distance runners, with bursts of speed of about 95 km/h (60 mph), and the ability to maintain speeds in excess of 50 km/h (31 mph) for distances of several kilometres.

Herds

Many ungulates, such as antelope and zebra, live in herds. This can provide greater safety, especially when there are young animals in the herd. The young can run within minutes of being born, which is essential to escape from predators.

The African savannah is home to many different types of ungulates, all living close together. They can do this because they feed on different foods so they do not compete with each other. Some graze on grass, while others browse on low shrubs or tall trees. The smaller antelopes, for example, feed on the lower branches of trees and on shrubs, while the giraffe can reach the higher branches.

Migrating

Many ungulates migrate (move to another location) in search of food. From the Serengeti plain in Tanzania, huge herds of wildebeest and zebra move north to find fresh grazing in Kenya. They have to cross wide rivers on their way, and some of the herd are drowned or killed by crocodiles in the water. Later in the year the herds return to the Serengeti. In North America, herds of caribou migrate north to find summer grazing in the Arctic, and then migrate back to the shelter of the forests for the winter.

Its long tongue, neck and legs allow the giraffe (*Giraffa camelopardalis*) to feed on the upper branches of acacia trees. A giraffe's tongue can grow up to 45 cm (18 in) long.

Desert survival

The camel is adapted to life in the desert. It has a hump containing fat stores and it can survive for weeks without water because of its amazing metabolism. It allows its body temperature to rise by a few degrees during the day and this means it reduces the amount of water it loses because it does not have to sweat. When it is very hot the camel sits with its rear end facing the sun. Only a small surface is exposed to the sun so it absorbs less heat. Deserts can be very cold at night so the camel loses heat. By morning its body temperature has fallen back to normal.

Arctic cold

Reindeer are found on the bleak Arctic plains and in the surrounding forest area. They have adapted to this freezing winter climate. They live in herds, which range in size from about 20 animals to several thousand. The herds are constantly on the move looking for food. They eat lichens, tough grasses and the leaves of low-growing trees. In winter they dig through the snow to find lichen and moss.

Huge herds of wildebeest (*Connochaetes taurinus*) have to cross rivers when migrating. During the river crossing many are attacked by crocodiles, and calves can be washed away in the strong river currents.

41

UNDER THREAT

MANY SPECIES OF MAMMALS ARE UNDER THREAT AROUND the world. It is possible that well-known animals such as the tiger, snow leopard, giant panda and rhino could be extinct in the wild within the next 30 years.

Loss of habitat

The main reason for the decline in mammal numbers is loss of habitat. As the human population gets larger, more land is needed and more habitats are lost. Habitats such as forest, grassland and even desert are being cleared to make more space for houses, factories and roads. Grassland is ploughed up and replaced by farmland. Trees are felled for timber and fuel. One of the world's most important habitats is the tropical rainforest. This habitat is home to more species of animals and plants than any other habitat. Sadly these valuable forests are being cleared at an ever-increasing rate and the homes of the tiger, jaguar, Asian elephant, gorilla, orang-utan and other mammals are disappearing.

This shop is selling tiger skins and a variety of medicinal products, some of which come from endangered animals.

Pollution can damage habitats, too. Air pollution from cars and factories can create acid rain, which kills trees. Water can be polluted by raw sewage, chemicals and oil spills. This harms marine mammals such as dolphins, seals and sea otters.

Hunting

Many mammals are hunted for their fur, tusks or horns. Snow leopards and other cats, bears and foxes are shot to make expensive fur coats. Elephants are killed for their ivory tusks, and rhinos for their horns. International laws have stopped the trade in ivory and in many furs, but the killing still continues illegally. Tigers are killed because some people believe that their bones and organs have medicinal value.

Success stories

Some mammals have been saved from extinction. The gray whale is no longer classed as an endangered animal because its numbers have increased. The golden lion tamarin from the South American rainforest has been bred in zoos and some have been released back into the rainforest. Przewalski's horse once roamed the plains of central Asia but it became extinct in the wild. Fortunately some survived in zoos, where they have bred successfully and there are now plans to reintroduce the horses to their old habitats. However, these captive-breeding schemes can only work if the animal's habitat is protected. If its habitat disappears, it can never be reintroduced back into the wild.

In 1980 there were fewer than 100 golden lion tamarins (*Leontopithecus rosalia rosalia*) left in the world. Now there are more than 1,000.

Mammal Classification

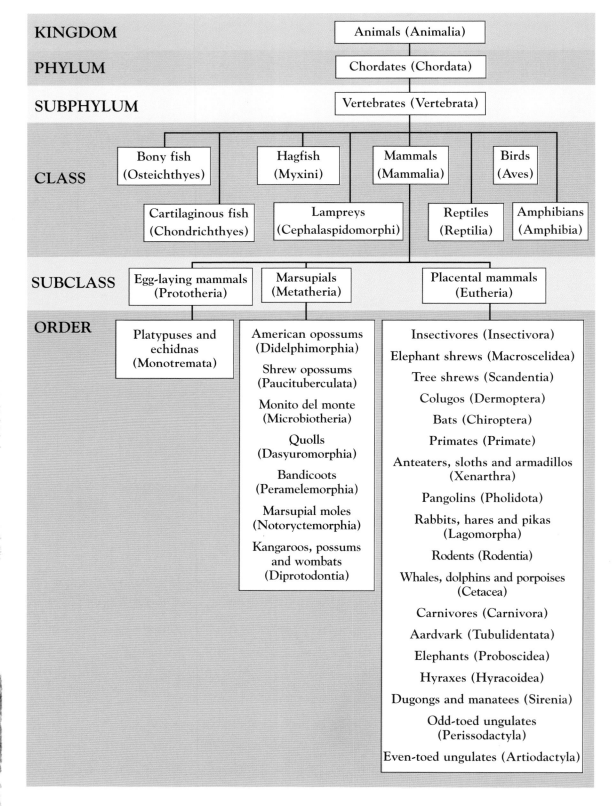

KINGDOM			Animals (Animalia)		
PHYLUM			Chordates (Chordata)		
SUBPHYLUM			Vertebrates (Vertebrata)		
CLASS	Bony fish (Osteichthyes)	Hagfish (Myxini)	Mammals (Mammalia)	Birds (Aves)	
	Cartilaginous fish (Chondrichthyes)	Lampreys (Cephalaspidomorphi)	Reptiles (Reptilia)	Amphibians (Amphibia)	
SUBCLASS	Egg-laying mammals (Prototheria)	Marsupials (Metatheria)	Placental mammals (Eutheria)		
ORDER	Platypuses and echidnas (Monotremata)	American opossums (Didelphimorphia)	Insectivores (Insectivora)		

ORDER (Marsupials):
- American opossums (Didelphimorphia)
- Shrew opossums (Paucituberculata)
- Monito del monte (Microbiotheria)
- Quolls (Dasyuromorphia)
- Bandicoots (Peramelemorphia)
- Marsupial moles (Notoryctemorphia)
- Kangaroos, possums and wombats (Diprotodontia)

ORDER (Placental mammals):
- Insectivores (Insectivora)
- Elephant shrews (Macroscelidea)
- Tree shrews (Scandentia)
- Colugos (Dermoptera)
- Bats (Chiroptera)
- Primates (Primate)
- Anteaters, sloths and armadillos (Xenarthra)
- Pangolins (Pholidota)
- Rabbits, hares and pikas (Lagomorpha)
- Rodents (Rodentia)
- Whales, dolphins and porpoises (Cetacea)
- Carnivores (Carnivora)
- Aardvark (Tubulidentata)
- Elephants (Proboscidea)
- Hyraxes (Hyracoidea)
- Dugongs and manatees (Sirenia)
- Odd-toed ungulates (Perissodactyla)
- Even-toed ungulates (Artiodactyla)

GLOSSARY

adapt To change over time in order to cope with the environment.

amphibious An animal that is adapted to living on both land and in water.

anatomy Parts of the body.

aquatic Living in water.

baleen plates Fibrous plates growing from the roof of the mouth of some species of whale, used to filter food from the water.

blubber A layer of fat just beneath the skin of marine mammals such as whales and seals, which traps heat in the body.

brachiation The name given to the way the gibbon moves through trees, swinging from one arm to the next.

breaching Jumping out of water by a whale.

bubonic plague A disease spread by rats' fleas, which causes fever and a painful swelling of the lymph glands.

canine tooth A tooth found near the front of the mouth, between the incisors and premolars. Most mammals have four canine teeth.

carnivore An animal that hunts and eats other animals. Also a member of the order Carnivora.

clot To congeal or stick together.

digest To break down food into simple substances that can enter the body.

diurnal Active in the daytime.

drey The name given to the nest of the squirrel.

echolocation To locate objects using sound.

endangered At risk of becoming extinct.

endothermic Animals such as mammals and birds, which have a high body temperature maintained by heat given off by the cells of the body.

evolved Changed over time.

extinct No longer in existence.

filter To sieve small particles from a liquid.

flipper The modified forearm of a seal or whale that helps it to swim.

habitat The place where an animal or plant lives.

herbivore An animal that eats plant foods.

hibernation A long, deep winter sleep.

incisors The small teeth found at the front of the mouth.

ivory The enamel of teeth, used to describe the tusks of elephants and walruses.

krill Shoals of small crustaceans that are found in the upper layer of the oceans, the favourite food of whales.

lichen An organism consisting of an alga and fungus living together.

mammal An animal that is covered in hair and has a constant body temperature. Female mammals produce milk for their young.

marsupial A mammal that gives birth to tiny young, which finish their development in a pouch.

matriarch The female leader of a herd of elephants.

GLOSSARY

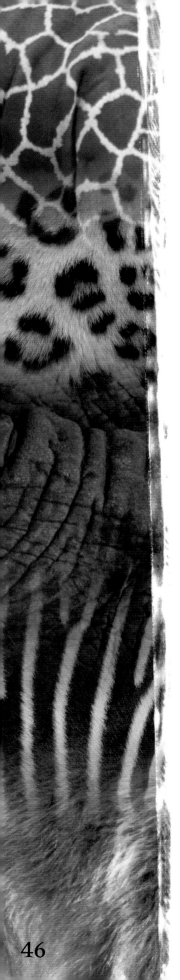

metabolism Chemical reactions that take place in living organisms, which provide energy.

migrate To make a regular journey between two different places at certain times of the year.

molar A large tooth at the back of the mouth, often used for chewing and grinding food.

monotreme An egg-laying mammal such as the platypus and echidna.

nectar The sugary fluid produced by flowers.

nocturnal Active at night.

omnivore An animal that eats a diet of plant and animal foods.

opportunist An animal that takes advantage of situations.

opposable thumb/toe A thumb or big toe that sticks out at an angle to the fingers or toes and allows the gripping and manipulation of objects.

parasite An organism that lives on or in another organism and causes that organism harm.

pest An animal that is present in large numbers and causes damage to crops.

placental mammal An animal that has a placenta. The placenta connects a baby to its mother in the uterus (womb). It carries food and oxygen from the mother to the baby.

plankton Tiny organisms that float in water.

pod A group of whales.

predator An animal that hunts and eats other animals.

prehensile Being able to wrap around objects, for example the trunk of an elephant and the tail of a monkey.

prey An animal that is hunted by a predator.

rabies A viral disease that affects the central nervous system.

regurgitate To bring up undigested food from the stomach back to the mouth to chew again.

reintroduce To release an animal back into its habitat.

ruminant A mammal that has a specialized stomach adapted to digesting grass and other plant foods.

savannah A grassland habitat with a few trees found in tropical parts of Africa.

scavenge To feed on the bodies of dead animals.

sp. An abbreviation for 'species', used as part of the Latin name for animals where the exact species is unknown.

species A kind of organism with unique features that are different from all other organisms, for example the African elephant or blue whale.

streamlined Having a shape that slips easily through the water.

tail fluke The two horizontally flattened parts of the tail of a whale, which are moved up and down to give propulsion through the water.

tapetum A layer within the eye.

vertebrate An animal that has a backbone, for example fish and mammals.

FURTHER INFORMATION

Books

100 Things You Should Know About: Mammals by Jinny Johnson (Miles Kelly Publishing, 2004)

1000 Things You Should Know About: Mammals by Steve Parker & Duncan Brewer (Miles Kelly Publishing, 2002)

21st Century Debates: Endangered Species by Malcolm Penny (Hodder Wayland, 2003)

Animal Classification by Polly Goodman (Hodder Wayland, 2004)

Animal Kingdom: Mammals by Sally Morgan (Raintree, 2004)

Classifying Living Things: Classifying Mammals by Andrew Solway (Heinemann Library, 2003)

DK Animal Encyclopedia (Dorling Kindersley, 2000)

The Encyclopedia of Animals: Mammals, Birds, Reptiles, Amphibians editors Forshaw, Gould and McKay (Fog City Press, 2002)

Life of Mammals by David Attenborough (BBC Books, 2002)

Life Processes series: *Classification* by Holly Wallace (Heinemann Library, 2002)

Living Nature: Mammals by Angela Royston (Chrysalis Children's Books, 2003)

Nature Files series: *Animal Groupings* by Anita Ganeri (Heinemann Library, 2003)

The New Encyclopedia of Mammals editor David Macdonald (Oxford University Press, 2001)

Science Answers: Classification by Richard & Louise A. Spilsbury (Heinemann Library, 2004)

Visual Encyclopedia of Animals by Barbara Taylor (Dorling Kindersley, 2000)

The Wayland Book of Common British Mammals by Shirley Thompson (Hodder Wayland, 2000)

Weird Wildlife: Mammals by Jen Green (Chrysalis Children's Books, 2003)

Websites

The Animal Diversity Web
http://animaldiversity.ummz.umich.edu
A huge site covering all the animal groups, compiled by the staff and students at the Museum of Zoology, University of Michigan.

BBC Nature
http://www.bbc.co.uk/nature/animals/mammals/
Video clips, facts and interactive challenges to show how mammals are so spectacularly successful.

Hall of Mammals at the University of California
http://www.ucmp.berkeley.edu/mammal/mammal.html
Website looking at all the different types of mammals including extinct ones such as the quagga.

The Mammal Society
http://www.abdn.ac.uk/mammal/
Fact sheets and an interative zone.

INDEX

Page numbers in **bold** refer to a photograph or illustration.